DEAR FR[...]

'Poems of exceptional grace[...]
—Fiona Sam[...]

'*Dear Friend(s)* takes on poetry's big subjects: sex, love and death, with an explosive panache. Formally and linguistically daring, these poems range from elegies written in the shadow of AIDS to tender love lyrics that offer both hope and healing. A gloriously original contribution to the growing canon of queer poetry.'
—Jacqueline Saphra

'Balancing survivor's guilt with Whitmanesque strains of wonder, *Dear Friend(s)* is that rare thing—an elegy which engages with the potential failure of the elegy but ultimately goes on to revivify it; to 'bring dead things to straining throats'. From the fireflies with their 'savage air', to the young man's beard, 'a biologically dead thing... marveled at', to the spring lambs, 'shreds of wool on wire barbs', Sugarman's is a poetic landscape of loss cut through with intense heat and longing.'
—Richard Scott

DEAR FRIEND(S)

By Jeffery Sugarman

To K—
What to say? I love
your poems & your spirit
you just works for poets.
Thanks for your
friendship!
Enjoy!

16/4/17

PS. T too (2) I love you!

THE EMMA PRESS

For Alan, my dearest

ℭℛ

In memoriam
My parents, Samuel and Marilyn Sugarman,
Lilly Mae White, Julienne Newham
&
Thomas Jahrling

THE EMMA PRESS

First published in the UK in 2019 by the Emma Press Ltd

Poems copyright © Jeffery Sugarman 2019

Edited by Charlotte Geater
Typeset by Emma Wright, in 18 pt Adobe Caslon Pro and 11.2 pt Minion Pro

ISBN 978-1-912915-18-7

A CIP catalogue record of this book
is available from the British Library.

Printed and bound in the UK
by Impact Print & Design, Hereford.

The Emma Press
theemmapress.com
hello@theemmapress.com
Birmingham, UK

CONTENTS

Between Dunes and Sea

still I'm in it
taunted by firelight
on water
wanting only heat

when all that is
is icy, and there
men like dinosaurs
blazoned in trinket waves

move through time
to me on the beach
the waves calling me
their cold

throwing me back
here at the edge of sand
and the men calling
too, their heat

and crash of ice
begun in a saltwash cradle
their tracks in the bedform
wash away

with each tremble wave
my hands held aloft
the creatures pass
age after age

their compass trace
scrapes beyond my palms
yet I reach, climb high
and only watch

still I'm in it

Vagus (The Wanderer)

So, It Started (at Home):
with orange blossom and the blistering sun.
Not paradise, entirely.

Lilly would clean, room by room—the living room,
the Florida Room, the hard tile floor in the kitchen—while I sat
and soaked in all the sadness of the house.
She'd pause to squeeze out the sponge
of me, and fill her deep, bright pail
with heavy, grey water.

Then the bedrooms—mine, with its sturdy bed,
but broken spring mattress, the stained sheets
she cleaned daily: no words spoken. No sign.

When time came to drive her home I'd be waiting
to jump in the car next to her and travel across town; to watch
those long, slow freight trains that seemed to go on forever—
    seemed to stop
everything from moving to the other side.

My father, he always signed his letters
                —Your devoted father

Mother? Well, in Lilly's words—
            Now Lord, ain't she a handful

You Can (Also) Start Here:
Lilly's shadowed-lawn, at home, where she worked,
after work, taking refuge out of the Florida heat,
grew her brilliant orange lilies
under the jasmine and live oaks;
a bed of blue plumbago—

Then there were the signs *Stay Off the Lawn*—
                    No Coloreds or Jews Allowed

Begin Again.

Here: 58th and 3rd—late light, silver on the windows of the
Empire State... a contralto practicing 'Resurrection' on the 4th
floor of a tenement... the tough in a blue serge suit, looking
back... fire engine geraniums, a solitary window box catching fire

Frankincense and Pelargonium.
Jasmine absolute.

Breathe!

Then, Lavender and Eucalyptus: moths

devouring the fabric, the embroidered words—
in my head, the train... the train of thought...

Then, Now, Here: and so it goes...

A bed (again)—your bed,
my lover's bed this time

so gentle: gentle then—
and repeatedly you

lay down atop me, press
your hands against my belly
and lift me up—an indigo
gecko leaps—fragrance
of anise

Now Here: it was bright and quite cold most of the morning
(after some overnight rain), now it's gone grey. You know how
that makes me!

But lovely robins and jays darting in and out of the patio, light
(now gone) shining
through the red-orange tulips! On fire like a dog's dick, red as a
lit candle... Now,

clouds: you never say *I love you*, not full-volume
rather a gesture, a reflex antiphony

But Wait (it took a long while for me to get it): you needn't say it,
not when hurrying me to bed like a sheepdog nipping at my
heels when it's late,
very late; or doing my laundry (pretending I don't know how,
that Lilly hadn't taught me
everything); or just calling me *jelly*

Stop Here Then: Gently

Dear Friend,

I am writing this   to you. No.
I am writing this   for us.
If you're there   please listen.
No echoes.   No woofs—
                         it's winter now

and the world's shut down. Our half of it,
that is, or—here. Silence all around
but for the urge. Where are you?
Where—the fuck are you? (All of you.)

*

Which of the cats ambling in my garden's warmth today
is you? Which hummock
your grave? What grass
shields those once-soft curls, the flesh?

In which hospital did you die, which room—
or was it hospice? Who wept
in that city of Presidents we loathed? I went
quiet: the escape—
                   it wasn't from you.

Orpheus,
I've dared to look back.

*

For it's how I wanted you—
in the photos; as in—
what I'd have said

if it weren't all so terribly
hidden
or lost.

We bent our bodies
blindly—couldn't imagine secrets
blooming like lesions. That spring,
as in any other year, fruit trees laden
with flowers, the bees crazed with hunger, some
falling like sharp tears—but innocence,
it really has nothing to do with this.

*

Dear Tom,

Your father won't know you, won't want to
the way I did. And him, I didn't know him
either—except what he filled you with, what you became; and
    though he'd never admit it
filled your mother with the seed to rear up that beautiful trunk.
    Native, crimson—
you made a fire of me, more than any man I'd ever touched; and
    you were good
as a cool damp towel on fire.

*

Dear Abundance

It's not the one photo I see, but accumulation
of 'Events'—

The beginning
Other days
Many more of the same

I skim them in search of some reason
some face I remember—
like a glistening
of squid in sunlit water

at their sudden turning
of a season from sharp bright frost
into narcissus or a shower
first thing in the morning
of falling stars burning out.

I'm drowning in abundance
where a knowing grin, a smile,
turns me like a top spinning too quickly;
in my head a pile of photos too high
      of you long ago—
      and you weren't gone.

The Photos folder is over-full
the hard drive still spinning

hours later—it can't find you
either.

*

(the turn)

This isn't a sonnet. (You knew what they were.)
Or even a song we'd have sung

badly—at the bar after work. But I've tried,
in the dark, and light, even the shower, early.

All this thinking: of abundance, absence,
for some potential. It's spring, you know—April,

and all that harshness—still, I remain shrouded
in leaf mould. But brilliant

yellow flower-heads and red-tipped golden cups
to hold aloft.

*

(Sonnet)

Water fell wildly—white and icy-cold—
through the narrow cleft, scoured the mountain,

each mica ridge, fissured and split, revealed
a deeper stone which embraced the pour.

Its after-flow was a bed of shards, the grass
having died long ago. In sunlight, the torrent

shone, as if an old man's beard—bristled,
grey and white, touched with darker hairs—rough

and irresistible as the younger lovers
of young men—until I wasn't. How

can it be that at such altitude the light
seems the same as by the sea, the sun

as hot, the longing just as profound, that
all fluids flow to the same water.

*

(other truths)

I wanted you, that's it, not all of it,
but true. Your bright torso; your
muscled thighs. What you wanted,
what you did with others' bodies, what
they did with you, only others know.
So, yes, lies.

*

(closing)

The problem is the world is just so beautiful
today—I had to.

All I wanted
was to sing you back.

But you'll have none of it—
not the Grindr hook-ups and more
bad elections; no nostalgia for haunted chatrooms.
The ease of bareback sex (after one week

of PrEP) or becoming husbands, for life,
if we choose. No mobile phones.

All this beauty: yours, the day's—
            it's a winter sky now, sharp-frosted
            and clear—
leaves me wanting. And all this singing,
this writing,
            it can't be about bringing you
back. There's so much to gain
in wanting.

*Note: "Tom" is Thomas W. Jahrling, born on February 12, 1957.
He died July 31, 1993, age 36. By the end of that year more than
360,000 cases of AIDS had been reported in the US with more
than 234,000 deaths.*

Fireflies (Hudson River Valley)

after Jean Valentine

i.

cars   at night   flash
flash red   fireflies   suspended

child, put down your glass cage   its *Ball* jar
lid.

ii.

in moonlight   oak wood and beech
the fires dance   air still   and vibratin

if I bled   it was not
like this.

iii.

savage air   garnet
quince

flames sheer   and pierced
heart, dream such fires.

iv.

freeway dawn   and dark   your promise
spent   the summer house   vanished

in liquid night
a torqued fire   rose.

Gallery

'...touching is not done with the fingers, but with a plectrum of ivory.'
—from *A Japanese Boy,* by Shiukichi Shigemi

I. MINIATURES

Sternum to glass
the boy listens: small birds
congregating out the window—
in storm gutters; branches
of small trees: acid tabebuia,
crepe myrtle barely budding.
The birds flit back and forth,
bring dead things
to straining throats;
their song
is quarrelsome.
The boy
is stiff
hidden
by nothing
as he looks.

> From another room, kitchen sounds and steam, smell of
> frying onions; then his father screaming *Serve it! I don't*
> *give a damn she's not home yet*—amidst the gentle tapping of
> spoons and pot lids; water running; Lilly Mae finishing the
> sauté pans: she and the table set for 5:30-sharp, routine—the
> embroidered tablecloth; cutlery engraved with an "S". Four
> places, 4-square on mahogany.

He is framed by a clutch of fine, ivory miniatures, by mostly-unknown painters; prim, meticulous, mostly-forgotten sitters—a solace to his father: their beauty, their oddity. And the painting "by Monet" (a small landscape, of quite pale watercolour); another by Utrillo. In the centre, the boy stares into blind light, wants simply for his mother to come home, to not lose control—of her legs, the car: what he fears most; wants the room not to be his harness—he gasps and puts a hand to the window, 5:30 sharp—

as so often before
she stays out
from her sickbed
glommed time for gossip
with salesgirls
and buying dresses
she's unlikely to wear—
to be closeted, unseen. But re-
hang the room: and
star-flare over waves,
pictures unframed, loosed
pigments
made flesh: re-
write the tale, I
tell him,
look again.

II. STILL LIFE WITH PEACOCKS

He looks to the surface of darkness   a room so deep
none sees through   Outside the fattened moon
faint in a burning sky   sings the lapping waves

where with dolphins   he'd learnt to swim   free
to dive great depths   not to be seen   as he is
in the dark   he can be heard breathing

should anyone stop   to listen   *Allí, caballero amigo*
a black tin knight   much older than he   stands guard
Their only light a nine-pointed   coloured-glass piñata

waiting to splinter into stars   a colourless TV
with plastic knobs   a bright-bolt of lightning
marked *Zenith*   There are petit-point headboards

his grandmother made   and quilting
to keep them warm at night .   winters brief
but bitter   beyond the shuttered windows   he knows

so well   give on to geckos   and sand-ants
a dense pointed-screen of palmetto   and a steep ladder
from which to drop down   his body

lithe   shade and colour of feather   its barbs
words etched in sand   no different
than the burnish of sun   brilliant as peacocks

III. Matryoshka

Deep in the dolls' nest, a babe, a man; hottest V-muscle, acuminate abdominal hair. Tiger line, treasure trail. Doll up, doll up... He smiles: he's not alone. Inside his pants—the wood grain and denim grain; veins

in his hand, vascular, expectant of course—always pressure to conceal. Zipper down and one eye: this time his, looking out whilst she, the requisite villain(ess), the mother (his mother—with something, lots

to say), rests in bed—as always. As always... The stone Venus: *La Grande Odalisque*—all the same: stone, which is not to say stones in a wall form a pattern, even like a pattern;

not even on paper (not really); nor a manner of shelter entire. Only the wall. No, the wall, and a shadow on it.

*

None of these images mattered (matter), of course, for there was only one: hers, adamantine. Her, eating a flabby poached egg each morning at nine—or noon... whenever she awakened, the same...

when she chose—on dry white toast touched with tears, the only salt she was allowed. Touched by salt and the gaze of a young man, now in jeans. Dolls away in the closet. But not away, not gone. Meanwhile,

on the beach where it's warm: there's sun and more star-flare than pictures on the wall. More blue than needly-leaves in the salt-cedar's sway—in the mild night air, the salt air, the westerlies here on the Gulf;

at sunset, as the air cools, as the wind picks up; and chases the sun. I will find him.

IV. Portrait as a Young Man

Staring in the mirror he considered the known thing before him: the beard he'd cared for since he was twenty; its deceptive solidity, the fullness of which he knew was no more than a massing of fine, fairly long hairs, colour of brass. It seemed his truer expression; the most visible and accurate manifestation of who he was. He tended it with a clinical fastidiousness, trimming it precisely—into a thing of beauty; he often considered each constituent thread a perfectly engraved line on a metal plate; the whole of it a polished armour, to shield and attract in equal measure.

He couldn't resist asking himself: had he carried the thing, this beard, or had it carried him—to this moment? A biologically dead thing he marveled at—hairs forced from follicles, out of necessity, to make room for something new. He'd grown, shaved and tended it, even though dead: it had power, grace; radiance even. Lovers had told him that—in the dark; had stroked it, growing hard; had admitted they wanted him for it, for that alone.

The Shepherd

Lambs: I think of shit—
shreds of wool on wire barbs, knots
that foul a hillside fence—colours of blood,
spring leaf, brown eternal mud—

restless, I wanted some fleeting ramshackle thing
rough, alternating with tender things

dull flecks that change in light; bright threads
that race and falter, go slack in fickle winds; torn scraps
of wool caught between sky and frozen ground,
streaming upwards to flocculent clouds—

meant takings: I wanted him prone
over me goading my silence

Lambs, fence-stuck and bloat-bleating,
loins heaving one side, head the other; the shepherd
promising, no, promised—if you obey
and love: salvation; immortality—

in shit, and worms
and the blue blue sky

The shepherd—he loves
and at night, holds, but doesn't take
or let me take; he knows I would, I'd take him,
as he knows thrawn ground breaks open

I would follow,
over bracken-covered fells and coursing rills; take the sheep track,
barely one footfall wide; or, switching back, find my own path
through matted grass and glossy stone; balance,
two-legs-as-one, upright as sheep;
and follow the smoke
to his hut...

A grown man now, well beyond lambing,
and grey, I write of a shepherd—the one in dreams,
who takes his charge from behind, by the horns,
small buds of spring

—not gently either.

The Buck Deer

after 'Skunk Hour' by Robert Lowell

The bull-headed buck, dark as wild cherry
is back, will not run or spook, stares,
unmoved by stones hurled in exasperation,
does not eat the pristine iris or lilies today
but mows the joints between our patio slates,
scours their surface for linden fruits and leaves—

Late afternoon
and the customary breeze is
up from the Sound, freshening the air,
has set the wind chimes off—their faint
Eastern song dissolving
in this chill summer's recent

heat; over it thrums a stereo,
"All in a dream…" I hear the season
fall in shadows across the lawn, return
to our rented cottage and close the door.
"The Sea Anchor," it's called by its lesbian owners:
they'd rather live in town.

The buck and herd return—I ask myself
had he saved the perennials for them?
They'd eaten our triumph tulips all spring,
like candy, coming from the small wood behind
where, now, vineyards are planned. July,
and the fields are a brown plaid.

The land's not right.

I see my own ill-spirit in it—summer's
easy hierarchies tightening; edges and margins
vanishing. Diatomaceous earth for the earwigs,
"liquid fence" for the deer and raccoons; Saabs
and organic farms—we've thrown dirt at the skies:
new stars worry the night...

Earth

where we kissed in a summer meadow rough grasses whipping
at our thighs sound of elk rutting in the distance where from
a sheer height the river's wash chill & flooding down we made
breathless descent the sun setting shadows on the rocks the
rocks indiscernible from our scuttered feet where we drove
for hours seeing nothing but scarred black stumps on pillow
stone and one bright sapling screaming green desert rocks
in countless layers seem soft felt in women's hands sprout
prickly pears and elk cows graze on roses in florid arid gardens
chrysanthemum smell of cum welling up within me—all I
want is to remain; there is no other than this earth to bear us
and so much yet unseen like a sudden flood through a slot
canyon when the earth says *go* we're gone

Lessons in Navigation

for my father-in-law, Douglas 'Owl' Newham, DFC
—RAF Bomber Command, Navigator 1941-1946

There are boys will split a bird
part from part,
its song silenced before dark.
The other birds watch

and sometimes mount a diversion.
Still the boys take another piece,
it doesn't matter which,
for spring. Speckled eggs

they'll smash in the schoolyard
before summer. By winter, a delicate
relief of bones   the butcher-boys march on
while others pull in their wings—

          Owl, how many nights,
and, oh, those miserable flights you survived
smoke and flame. Bright-winged men lost
and shattered across the world—
and the enemy.
          But Owl, here you are,
still sharp, soaring at ninety-five; nearer
to the end if I'm honest, and closer
to the ground. Still, you see thick layers of cloud
for what they are, colour and mist, changing
from nimbus to pearl, mostly;
             some days only lead,
death perhaps seeming reprieve.

　　　　　　　And, Owl, how many lessons
I've learnt—how alike we are (who's prey, and who
is preyed upon—each kind, not so kind: the same

choices to be taken). We must find our own
good way—

Owl, you've been with me some while
　　　　　　　　　now: I'm changed.

Lost Sonnet—for Julienne

In the photo she's in baggy pants, hands relaxed, and smiling,
an unaccustomed insouciance; the jeans a dirty blue, her hair
bright, but soon was only grey. And their home wild through—
rooms too small to hold her banging, of pans—

and stolen things, she said. They spoke still at dinner,
but less and less, over burnt roasts; and less still
was understood. She spoke loudly, became all fists
and thieves. How mightily he tried, offering kind words

and touches—for them. Once they had loved. But
she'd forgotten now, it was clear, to dust their holiday
trinkets and photos which she, too, had loved. This went
on, in shrinking houses and new surrounds till their days

were wrapped into a blinding. In care, her skin grew slack; hands
seemed to splinter in his grasp. The mind, at last, seemed still...

but lungs—a creaking bellows. Her body——— the thinnest line.
*

How long we take in dying—and, Julienne, lost long before:
a lifetime we're told after. After... what did he say?

It was days. And I
would hardly know her.

Animal Etudes

i.
He heard the green bird in his lungs again, felt it
rattle, and shake all the buildings around him; felt
he could keep the walls upright for his good neighbours,
that choking on the world's darkness, then speaking gently
was their only hope.

ii.
The call of the gulls this morning was shrill
and reassuring
in the bright winter light (we were some distance
from the sea
as the fog billowed in and the gulls' shrieks
subsided) maybe
because I'd spent so many years calling out.

iii.
I imagine myself the bird, the one
he'd imagined, but bright, eating seed,
the hearts of them—my own
tired muscle,
              just to touch it again
as when it was firm with fire.

iv.
But I just can't now, the animals
are furthest from my mind. Perhaps
ignoring the animal other, the one within me,
is the fault here.
        This is when my most cherished animal
creeps up behind me like the cats he loves

and drops a hot cup of mind-altering
tea on the coffee table—he loves irony—
behind me. Says, *let me write you a poem,*
'The Cat'.

v.
I turn from my meditation on compassion, practising first
   on myself, to relish "Ted
with Tires" in its cheap black frame against the wall, and
   other Herb Ritts delights.
Then another *tumbl* of men
from the screen on my desk. And there I wait
for his first draft.

vi.
The morning sun
and with it, birds. Then rain,
and no matter the time, the birds
mostly leave.

I'm sat here again
under the ringing-wet of a corrugated roof
and want nothing more than to cast hallelujahs
splattering into the sky, or several etudes
approximating it… a Mahler symphony.
No matter the clef or key. An opening
in the book of infinite rehearsal.

But, no, I'm writing
and re-writing the morning
as on any ordinary day

it shines *How lucky I am*
how you don't mind, maybe
even understand
I'll sit here until dark,
and it's not raining, when their chatter,
more raucous, brash this time, returns.

vii.
Those cats, carrying in them so many bodies, the souls
of lost friends, lovers, men with undisclosed names.
Those cats, those tricksters: I don't mean to get all crazy here
with spirituality, so let's just call them memories, so porous,
so lithe up in the garden, those cats. I can't look at them now,
perhaps because I can't see them without seeing you
dead someday, not this day, but I've a devious mind, it likes to anticipate
life in fantastic ways, and, yes,
sometimes, most times it seems,
storms, wounds of the flesh
and souls, there, those souls again, those sweet
cats that move with the elegance of you inside me.

Ascent to Orchids in the Morning

I'm leaving he calls down to me,
and I run up from my desk, as I do
most days, to catch him at the door.

Not so fast that I might slip on the stair
or appear too eager; a gentle pace
is an English pace, that's what I've learnt.

I straighten his collar
the way he straightened mine
when we first met, give him a peck

on the cheek and send him off.
Then walk slowly to the top of the house
all lit up with a milky sun,

a small lantern of a room,
a bath, and above it
a skylight, large enough

to see the stars at night, of this galaxy
(at least) and beyond. And the orchids.
A dozen of them. They've come back,

not perfectly or without exception, but new leaves
and flower stalks beneath, just sprouting,
easily mistaken for aerial roots. So I've blunted a few.

Above the skylight, a row of chimney pots,
their cowls still slowly moving. The morning
is changing. The sky is something not yet

blue, but frames two spring-birds
spiralling headstrong for the ground.
I've climbed as far in this Georgian house

from my dungeon mind as I can go. The stairs,
the stars and the birds in love. My English husband
walking out, and later, returning. Chimney cowls

last night howling in a gale: hell laying claim
to the morning. But the morning, it's mine,
and I can take a bath with orchids.

ACKNOWLEDGEMENTS

Thanks to my many dear friends, some addressed directly in these poems, for their encouragement and inspiration; and to the institutions and tutors who have supported me over many years. Chief among them are the Fine Arts Work Center in Provincetown, MA, (USA), and The Hurst, Arvon Centre, in Shropshire (UK); and the poets I met and worked with there: Mark Doty, Carl Phillips, Alan Shapiro, Marie Howe, and, especially, Ada Limón for her invaluable guidance and insight over the last 3 years, at the former; and at The Hurst, Jacqueline Saphra and Fiona Sampson, without whom this collection would still be a dream.

More recently, I'm grateful to Richard Scott for the inspiration of his poems and warm friendship, Katy Evans-Bush for careful reading of this manuscript and Kathryn Maris and my fellow APW poets at the Poetry School in London.

Special thanks to The Emma Press: Emma Wright for her indomitable commitment, and wonderful cover illustration; to Rachel Piercey for early encouragement; and especially my editor, Charlotte Geater, who had the confidence and patience to see these poems into print.

ABOUT THE POET

Jeffery Sugarman is an American-born poet living in London. He grew up in 1960s Florida when the state was still relatively untrammelled, a bit exotic—swampy, bursting with coconut palms, peacocks and mermaids; shaded by live oaks, draped with grey moss. He moved to Philadelphia for studies at the University of Pennsylvania, then the University of Virginia, Charlottesville, for a graduate architecture degree, continuing northward after to Washington, DC, and New York. He has written in various forms all his life: first, architecture and design criticism; then in planning and urban design in his career spanning over 20 years in New York City, where he lived, and began writing poetry, from the mid-1990s. He moved to London in 2009 with his English husband, and lives on Islington's 'west-side'.

Jeffery's work has been published or is forth-coming in *Here-There Poetry*, *Magma* and *American Book Review*, and long-listed in the National Poetry Competition 2016. He is a 2019-20 Jerwood/ Arvon mentee working with Hannah Lowe; and reads in venues throughout London. *Dear Friend(s)* is his debut collection.

ABOUT THE EMMA PRESS

The Emma Press is an independent publisher dedicated to producing beautiful, thought-provoking books. It was founded in 2012 by Emma Wright in Winnersh, UK, and is now based in the Jewellery Quarter, Birmingham.

The Emma Press publishes poetry and fiction anthologies and pamphlets for adults and for children, with a growing list of translations.

The Emma Press has been shortlisted for the Michael Marks Award for Poetry Pamphlet Publishers in 2014, 2015, 2016 and 2018, winning in 2016.

theemmapress.com
emmavalleypress.blogspot.co.uk